Scientists
IN ACTION

ARCHAEOLOGISTS IN ACTION

CRABTREE
PUBLISHING COMPANY
WWW.CRABTREEBOOKS.COM

Megan Kopp

Author: Megan Kopp

Series research and development: Reagan Miller

Editorial director: Kathy Middleton

Photo research: James Nixon

Editors: Paul Humphrey, James Nixon, Janine Deschenes, Reagan Miller

Proofreader and indexer: Lorna Notsch

Designer: Keith Williams (sprout.uk.com)

Prepress technician: Samara Parent

Print coordinator: Katherine Berti

Layout: Keith Williams (sprout.uk.com)

Consultant: Brianne Manning

Produced for Crabtree Publishing Company
by Discovery Books

Cover image: An archaeologist in Lima, Peru uncovers
remains of dogs and guinea pigs

Photographs:

Alamy: pp. 8 (Granger Historical Picture Archive); 10
(ZUMA Press, Inc.); 11 (Keith Morris); 13 top (Robert
Harding); 14 (Jim Gibson); 15 top (Sergio Azenha); 16
(Horizons WWP/TRVL); 18 (David Hilbert); 20 (dpa
picture alliance archive); 23 top (Eddie Gerald); 28
(RosaIreneBetancourt 14); 29 (Chad Chase)

Archaeology in the Community: p. 21 bottom

Getty Images: cover (ERNESTO BENAVIDES/AFP)

Hakai Institute: title page left, p. 13 bottom (Grant
Callegari)

Parks Canada: p. 7 (Thierry Boyer)

Shutterstock: pp. 5 bottom (Patricia Hofmeester); title page
middle, 9 top (Efired); 12 (Salvador Aznar); 17 (Daan
Kloeg); 19 top (lexar001); 22 (Rafal Cichawa)

Wikimedia: pp. 9 bottom; 19 bottom (Boston Public Library
Tichnor Brothers collection); title page top right, 21 top
(Wellcome Images)

All other images from Shutterstock

Library and Archives Canada Cataloguing in Publication

Kopp, Megan, author
    Archaeologists in action / Megan Kopp.

(Scientists in action)
Includes index.
Issued in print and electronic formats.
ISBN 978-0-7787-4645-4 (hardcover).--
ISBN 978-0-7787-4654-6 (softcover).--
ISBN 978-1-4271-2058-8 (HTML)

    1. Archaeology--Juvenile literature. 2. Archaeologists--Juvenile
literature. I. Title.

CC171.K67 2018   j930.1   C2017-907807-0
                                        C2017-907808-9

Library of Congress Cataloging-in-Publication Data

CIP available at the Library of Congress

Crabtree Publishing Company

www.crabtreebooks.com   1-800-387-7650

Printed in the U.S.A./052018/CG20180309

Published in Canada
Crabtree Publishing
616 Welland Ave.
St. Catharines, Ontario
L2M 5V6

Published in the United States
Crabtree Publishing
PMB 59051
350 Fifth Avenue, 59th Floor
New York, New York 10118

Published in the United Kingdom
Crabtree Publishing
Maritime House
Basin Road North, Hove
BN41 1WR

Published in Australia
Crabtree Publishing
3 Charles Street
Coburg North
VIC, 3058

CONTENTS

What Is Archaeology?   4

The Search for Answers   6

People Who Dig the Past   8

Scientific Practices   10

The Quest Begins with Questions   12

Site Surveys   14

Data Collection   16

Analyzing and Interpreting Data   18

Communication   20

Conservation and Collaboration   22

Dig It!   24

Projects and Discoveries   26

Getting Involved   28

Learning More   30

Glossary   31

Index & About the Author   32

WHAT IS ARCHAEOLOGY?

Whether it is a gold-filled burial chamber in Egypt, a small stone tool found on the Canadian prairies, or a shipwreck filled with statues, every discovery is a key to the past. It does not matter if the discovery is large or small. Each discovery helps unlock another time and place. It opens a door to understanding the past. Finding those keys is the work of a special field of science called archaeology.

Chaco Culture National Historical Park in New Mexico holds secrets dating back more than 1,000 years.

The word "archaeology" comes from a Greek word meaning *ancient*, or very old. Archaeology is the study of how people lived in the past. It is a field of science, that involves discovering ancient objects, examining them carefully, and explaining what they mean. In this book, you will discover the type of work archaeologists do and the questions they hope to answer. We will look closely at the scientific practices archaeologists use as they carry out investigations and make new discoveries about the past.

Hunting Artifacts

The ancient objects that people leave behind are called **artifacts**. Over hundreds and even thousands of years, dirt and rocks build up and bury artifacts. This buildup is called sediment. Archaeologists work hard to uncover and examine artifacts. Sometimes buried under meters of sediment, artifacts are found in a range of sizes and are made from many different materials. They are often broken or scattered. Artifacts are found on land—and even underwater—all over the world.

Artifacts, such as the point of a spear, are clues to unlocking stories from a buried past.

Myth Busting

Few archaeologists are like the movie versions of Indiana Jones in *Raiders of the Lost Ark* or Lara Croft in *Tomb Raider*. They do not all search for golden treasures or dig up **mummies**. That said, archaeological sites can be found almost anywhere in the world, including areas as diverse as the Canadian Arctic and the Mojave Desert in California.

Puzzle Masters

Uncovering artifacts and understanding the past are like putting together a jigsaw puzzle, only there is no clear picture to follow and some of the pieces will probably be missing. Archaeologists use scientific practices to study and investigate what others leave behind and to communicate their findings.

These archaeologists are carefully working at an ancient Roman fort and settlement in northern England.

THE SEARCH FOR ANSWERS

Archaeologists are always searching for answers to questions. Some questions are focused on specific details about the past. For example, an archaeologist might ask if an uncovered pot was once used for cooking or storing grain. Other archaeologists may search for answers to broader questions, such as where did a group of people come from originally and why did they choose an area to settle?

Finding a Focus

Within the field of archaeology, there are many different specialties. The field is often divided into time periods and regions, or areas, studied. For example, **prehistoric** archaeology deals with time periods before writing was invented. Historical archaeology, such as that done on American Civil War battlefields, involves looking at artifacts found in the field and written records taken from **archives** and libraries. Classical archaeology specializes in examining ancient Greek and Roman **civilizations**. Mesoamerican archaeology focuses on Central American and Mexican **cultures**. Post-classic archaeology covers cultures in the Americas since 1200 C.E., such as the Incas.

Environmental archaeology looks at the past relationships in nature between plants, animals, and people. **Industrial** archaeology studies the remains of buildings and equipment used in industry. There is even the archaeology of garbage, or garbology. Scientists can learn a lot about a society by studying the material it discards.

Machu Picchu is an ancient Inca city discovered in Peru more than 100 years ago, but archaeologists are still trying to fully understand its purpose.

Underwater Archaeology

In 1845, explorer Sir John Franklin left England on an expedition to what is now Canada's Arctic. He was looking for a northern sea route from the Atlantic Ocean to the Pacific Ocean. The expedition's two ships, HMS *Erebus* and HMS *Terror* became trapped in ice. None of the crew survived. Marc-André Bernier is the manager of Parks Canada's Underwater Archaeology team. In 2014, his team discovered the sunken wreck of the *Erebus*. Two years later they found the *Terror*. A few artifacts have been recovered, but it will take years of study to uncover the fate of the doomed crew.

The damaged remains of HMS Erebus *are explored during short periods of favorable weather in the icy Arctic.*

Uncover, Protect, Preserve

Many archaeologists hope to uncover artifacts that will help them answer questions about who once lived in an area and when they lived there. They may hope to understand how people lived and why. They often work at digs in this area to carefully uncover artifacts from the past to provide answers to their research questions. Other archaeologists may work to protect or preserve artifacts, or other **cultural resources**, such as old buildings and ruins, that remain on or in the ground today. They may work in parks or other protected sites to ensure people do not damage these resources. Or, they may be involved in protecting cultural resources in areas where building projects are planned.

PEOPLE WHO DIG THE PAST

People have examined prehistoric sites and collected artifacts for thousands of years. The earliest people who did this were not scientists, but thieves and grave robbers looking to make money by selling artifacts or add to their personal collections of artifacts. Archaeologists value artifacts not as possessions, but as important pieces of **evidence** that may help answer questions about the past. They carefully describe each artifact and monitor exactly where it was found, so that future generations can use their research.

Treasures in the Tomb

Professional archaeologists live and work all around the world. Sometimes we are more familiar with the discoveries than we are with the archaeologists who first uncovered them. Howard Carter was a famous British archaeologist. In 1922, Carter uncovered King Tutankhamun's grave. Unlike many other Egyptian tombs, Tutankhamun, had never been discovered by grave robbers. Carter found close to 5,000 artifacts in the tomb, including other mummified bodies and a solid gold coffin.

Howard Carter and his assistant examine the remains of King Tutankhamun.

Kenyan Louis Leakey and his British-born wife Mary were **paleoanthropologists** and archaeologists. They studied prehistoric people. The Leakeys are known for their amazing **fossil** discoveries in Tanzania, Africa, in the 1960s. Mary and Louis Leakey's fossil finds were important in understanding human **evolution** and **migration**. Thanks to their work, archaeologists now believe that humans first evolved in Africa before migrating to different places on Earth.

Archaeologists believe there are more than 8,000 clay soldiers in the Terracotta Army.

Developing Technology

The Terracotta Army is part of a massive burial chamber built for the first emperor, or ruler, of China. It was discovered by accident in 1974 when workers were digging a well. Over the next three years, archaeologists uncovered 800 warrior figures, 18 wooden chariots, and more than 100 pottery horses. In 1985, another **excavation** began, but it lasted less than a year. In the first two digs, the soldiers lost their color when exposed to air. In 2015, excavations started again. Newly developed technology allowed archaeologists to preserve the colors painted on the figures. The colors highlight expressions on the faces and could provide new insights into the study of ancient China.

From the Field: Flinders Petrie

British archaeologist Flinders Petrie began working in Egypt in 1880. He was among the first to take a scientific approach to archaeology. He took great care in recording all of his finds. Petrie was the first to match pottery types with different cultures and time periods. This allowed archaeologists to establish relatively accurate timelines for artifacts, before other dating methods were invented.

SCIENTIFIC PRACTICES

Scientific practices reflect the many ways in which scientists explore and understand the world. Scientists may not use all of the practices (see box). It depends on the science field and the question they are trying to answer. As in any field of science, archaeologists use scientific practices in the field and in the lab. It is not always a straightforward process. Some parts of the process may be repeated.

Scientific Practices

■ Asking questions

■ Developing methods of investigation, including building **models** and designing observations and experiments

■ Carrying out investigations

■ Analyzing and interpreting data collected

■ Using mathematics and technology to process data

■ Constructing explanations from evidence

■ Communicating findings and conclusions

In the lab, an archaeologist analyzes the animal bones she has collected.

What's the Theory?

Archaeologists studying the Ancestral Puebloan culture in southern Utah might ask why this culture disappeared. Was it because of drought? Was it because of warfare? Based on their own knowledge and additional research, archaeologists come up with an idea called a **hypothesis**. The archaeologists might believe the Ancestral Puebloan culture suffered from a combination of changing climate, a shortage of food, and warfare with other tribes who threatened to steal their resources. A plan is constructed to test this complicated hypothesis.

What's the Answer?

Archaeologists use the plan to gather evidence, or data, from a site. They look carefully at all of the data collected. This is called **analysis**. Careful observation and analysis are vital steps in archaeology. These are the basis for discussion and interpretation of the results. This may create new questions.

The archaeologists use the data to see if it supports their original hypothesis. Eventually, the artifacts and the information obtained from the dig are communicated to others. Archaeologists may communicate their findings to other archaeologists and to the public through such things as articles, talks, and museum displays.

How Old Is an Artifact?

An important step in the process of archaeology is to figure out the age of artifacts. Stratigraphy is the analysis of the layers of soil and rock at an archaeological site. The oldest layer of soil and rock is usually at the bottom. The youngest is on top. Archaeologists can analyze the layers of rock and soil at a dig site to determine their general ages, and then date an artifact based on the layer in which it was found.

Carbon-14 is a chemical found in all living things. So, for example, when a tree dies, the amount of carbon-14 in its cells decreases at a set rate over time. An artifact made from wood can be tested for carbon-14. It helps archaeologists tell the age of that artifact.

Layers of soil and rock can help archaeologists date artifacts found in old settlements.

THE QUEST BEGINS WITH QUESTIONS

The first step in archaeology is to consider questions about the past that might be answered by researching archaeological dig sites. A question can be as straightforward as how did people in a particular area hunt deer 2,000 years ago? It also might be a more complex question, such has how did the earliest people arrive in North America?

Preparing to Dig

Research from historical sources, previous digs, and published papers can help archaeologists form questions. These questions become the basis of a new investigation. Archaeologists write their hypotheses and propose ways in which their investigation will try to find the answers. A research proposal is a plan for the dig.

For example, aarchaeologists focused on the history of **trade** between ancient peoples might examine research on foreign artifacts found in Italy. Based on previous discoveries of pottery made in Greece in some parts of Italy, the archaeologist might ask whether people in a certain region of Italy traded with the Greeks. The archaeologists would propose how and where to dig in Italy and the evidence of pottery from Greece they hope to find. Proposals are necessary because they guide the research archaeologists do, and can also be submitted to receive **funding** for the project.

Data collected from this ancient archaeological site in Rome, Italy, will be analyzed and interpreted by the archaeologists in the hope of finding answers to their questions.

Digging Archaeology

Archaeological digs are well-planned. Excavations are often constrained by time and money. The sites are rare and valuable and normally only investigated once. Archaeologista do not dig at random and hope they find data to support their hypotheses. They need to have a clear picture of what they are looking for and where best to find it. Test pits are often dug by archaeologists to see if the location chosen is good before a full-scale dig begins. Sometimes, only a small portion of a dig site is uncovered. Other areas are left unexcavated for future archaeologists to one day investigate with different, more advanced scientific tools and methods.

Archaeologists use soft paintbrushes to wipe soil off fragile artifacts without damaging them.

The ancient village found at Triquet Island is three times as old as the Great Pyramid of Giza in Egypt and among the oldest human settlements in North America.

The First Peoples

"How did the first peoples reach North America?" is a question often asked by research archaeologists. Off the coast of British Columbia, archaeologists have uncovered an ancient village dating back 14,000 years—among the oldest human settlements in North America. Archaeologists from the University of Victoria's Hakai Institute, and the local Heiltsuk Nation discovered tools, animal bones, and other artifacts at the site on Triquet Island, 250 miles (400 km) northwest of Vancouver. Coastal sites like this support the hypothesis that the earliest people who arrived in North America settled along the coastline, traveling by boat.

SITE SURVEYS

Archaeologists begin planning their investigation by scanning a potential site. Sometimes this is done visually, by searching for pieces of pottery or other artifacts on the surface. Finds are marked with flags. Small test trenches may be dug in an area with a large number of flags. If there are additional buried artifacts, it will probably be a good place to excavate. This process is part of a site survey.

If the site looks promising, archaeologists will then carry out a **geophysical** survey to discover what lies under the ground. Machines that use electricity to test soil can reveal hidden walls and buildings. Magnetometry is the measurement and mapping of patterns of magnetism in soil. Things like stone walls and firepits leave magnetic traces that can be detected with special equipment. Archaeological features show up as having either lower or higher readings of magnetism than undisturbed areas around them.

An archaeologist uses a magnetometer in a geophysical survey in southern Scotland.

Bring out the Math

Once the location for the dig is established, a **transit** is used to map the site. All of the work starts from a set point on the ground. This is called a **datum point**. It never moves. The location of every find is measured from the datum point. This includes the distance horizontally and the distance vertically down from the datum point.

Once the site is mapped, a grid made up of wooden pegs and string is laid out over the site. Each section of the grid is usually one meter square, but this can vary. For underwater sites, a metal grid is used. Breaking the site into these smaller sections, called grid squares, allows archaeologists to precisely map found artifacts.

Down to Earth

Archaeologists must remove soil carefully to preserve the stratigraphic layers that they use for dating their finds. Sometimes large equipment is brought in to take off the top layers to reach the older layers beneath. Most of the excavation is done slowly and carefully, with a variety of hand tools and equipment, such as shovels and small trowels. Even tiny paintbrushes are used to avoid damaging fragile artifacts.

Using a grid made up of string, archaeologists can accurately record and map their findings.

The positions of the artifacts, including the layers of rock and soil at which they were found, are recorded on a map. The artifacts are then brushed and cleaned, photographed, drawn, and recorded in notes. Important artifacts are numbered and put into bags for further study away from the site. At the end of the day, archaeologists, who often work as a team, get together to discuss what was uncovered and to decide how best to continue the dig on the following day.

Super Sight

Sites can be given an initial survey from the air without the need to touch the ground at all. Lidar (light detection and ranging technology) uses a giant laser scanner that is attached to the side of a helicopter or put in a plane. This scanner has the ability to see through dense vegetation. Using lidar, archaeologists can produce detailed three-dimensional (3-D) maps of Earth's surface. These maps help archaeologists build a picture of an archaeological site before a possible excavation. Ground-penetrating **radar** can also be used to record features below the surface.

Aerial views of sites can provide valuable information to archaeologists. For example, they may show areas of raised earth.

DATA COLLECTION

Data includes photos, maps, measurements, soil samples, artifacts, and notes that archaeologists gather during a dig. All of the data is carefully analyzed. Patterns are identified. These become evidence that proves whether or not a hypothesis is correct.

Archaeologists screen dirt from a dig site, searching for tiny pieces of artifacts.

An Eye for Detail

Archaeologists are trained to look for detail. The soil removed from a grid square is passed through fine screens to make sure no small seeds, bones, or pieces of pottery are missed. Archaeologists note changes in soil layers. Each new layer of soil belongs to a different period of time. Artifacts found at the bottom of a dig are normally older than those found in the top layers.

Why Is the Metric System Used?

Archaeologists and other scientists around the world use the metric system for measuring and reporting data. Even archaeologists in the United States measure artifact sizes in millimeters and centimeters rather than fractions of inches. Using a common measuring system allows archaeologists to share and understand one another's data no matter where they live.

Gathering as much information as possible puts everything into context. Context is how the artifacts relate to each other and to the environment in which they are found. Artifacts are dated by carbon-14 dating or by the approximate age of the soil layer they were found in. Other artifacts found in the same layer are assumed to be the same age.

Artifacts Tell a Story

Sometimes, where an artifact is found is not evidence of where it was made or first used. Many artifacts are found hundreds or thousands of miles from where they were made. Obsidian is a type of natural volcanic glass used to make sharp points for spears. Obsidian was traded across North America. Tracing obsidian artifacts across North America can show which peoples used spears for hunting and the places in which they lived. It is important to find as many pieces of the puzzle as possible to get a clear picture of what took place and how people lived.

Photographing Finds

Archaeologists collect information about artifacts through data. Photographs are important data collected at a dig site. Archaeologists use photographs to record the context of an artifact in a number of ways:

- Archaeologists create scale by placing something of known size beside an artifact. For example, a modern coin might provide scale for ancient coins found in the earth.

- Archaeologists capture context by taking pictures of the artifact's surrounding environment. They photograph any surrounding artifacts found.

- Archaeologists take photographs from different angles to get a total view of the artifact.

It is important to photograph artifacts where they were found before they are bagged and removed for further study. This ties the artifact to a particular place and soil layer in a dig site.

ANALYZING AND INTERPRETING DATA

When the dig is finished, the next phase of an archaeologist's job begins. What does it all mean? How do the pieces fit together to tell us something about life in the past? Artifacts taken from a dig site are carefully cleaned of debris in a lab. Sometimes they are pieced back together. The constructed piece might provide new information that individual pieces did not show.

One like Another

Archaeologists begin by studying each individual artifact. They look at its size, shape, material, and color. These are called **attributes**. Archaeologists can sort artifacts into groups based on these attributes. Groups can be arranged in many different ways. It could be by the materials from which they were made, or what archaeologists think the artifacts were used for. They make notes on how many similar pieces were found, where different types of artifacts were found, and how old they are.

Archaeologists make comparisons with similar objects that people use today. They study each individual piece from a site. All of the artifacts from a site are called an assemblage. Groups within the assemblage can show patterns. There might be a group of pots near a firepit. Their location hints that they were used for cooking. These patterns provide clues to how people lived in the past.

This assemblage of pottery provides insights into life in an ancient village in Oaxaca, Mexico.

Explaining the Data

More often than not, the evidence archaeologists interpret is incomplete. By studying the artifacts that were found within their context, archaeologists can also make hypotheses about artifacts that may be missing. They use all of this information to develop a theory about the dig as a whole. An excavation report is written to explain the story of the site based on what was found. This is an **interpretation** of the findings.

Archaeologists will interpret this site to explain why a person was buried here 3,500 years ago.

Finding the Pilgrims

The Pilgrims crossed the Atlantic on the *Mayflower* in 1620. They settled in Plymouth Colony. It was the first lasting English settlement in what is now the United States. The exact location of the colony was lost over time. In 2016, archaeologists discovered a 17th-century site in Massachusetts. They believed it was the original Plymouth settlement. How did they know? Pilgrims raised **domesticated** cattle. Bones of a calf were found at the site beneath a soil layer dating to before 1650. Archaeologists also found trade beads that were given to local tribes at the time in exchange for food or furs. These discoveries helped to confirm the age of the site.

COMMUNICATION

The scientific process of archaeology helps build a picture or story about the past. These stories need to be shared for many reasons. Sharing allows other archaeologists to input their thoughts and ideas. Sharing also invites the public to learn and care about the past.

The discoveries on an old battlefield, such as this head of an axe, are presented to the public.

Best Practices

There are many different ways to interpret data. **Peer** reviewing is an important step for archaeologists when preparing to communicate their findings. It is important that archaeologists share their work with peers to overcome **bias**. This is the perspective, or point of view, that an archaeologist brings to his or her investigation. Sometimes, that perspective can mean that the findings are interpreted or presented with bias. By sharing their findings, archaeologists can make sure that their personal perspectives are not changing how the investigation is analyzed or presented. Sharing their findings with peers can also help bring up points that may have been overlooked or ignored. Discussion improves the interpretation of the evidence gathered.

After an archaeologist has finished with the artifacts, they are catalogued in a computer database and stored. Some will be used for museum exhibits and others for educational programs. These collections are examined by researchers and can also be used as starting points for other archaeological research projects.

Archaeologists communicate their findings at the completion of an investigation. Publication of archaeological work is important. Sharing the work in **journals** and reading reports at **conferences** allows others to make connections with their own current and future work. Archaeologists can agree, disagree, or take an interpretation in a whole different direction.

Fake Finds

In 1912, English newspaper headlines proclaimed the discovery of a prehistoric skull by an amateur archaeologist named Charles Dawson. Dubbed the Piltdown Man, after the village near to where it was found, the remains were estimated to be between 500,000 and 1,000,000 years old. Archaeologists believed that Piltdown Man was the "missing link" in evolution between apes and humans. It turned out to be a hoax. In 1953, experts declared that the skull's braincase belonged to a modern human and the jawbone to an orangutan or chimpanzee (left). The pieces had been stained to match. The teeth were flattened with a metal file.

From the Field: Dr. Alexandra Jones

Dr. Alexandra Jones (right) is a community archaeologist. She works with schools and community groups, raising awareness and understanding of archaeology and history by sharing her passion for the subject. Community archaeologists provide hands-on exhibits and learning opportunities. These help people understand what archaeology is and how important it is to preserve the past. Jones founded a program called Archaeology in the Community in Washington, D.C. The program works with school groups and community members to share knowledge about archaeology.

CONSERVATION AND COLLABORATION

Why is archaeological conservation important? Archaeological resources are irreplaceable. Once damaged or destroyed, the knowledge these resources hold is lost forever.

In the early years of archaeology, it was normal for cultural treasures to be removed from a site and taken to a university or museum. The Elgin Marbles, for example, are a collection of ancient sculptures taken from the Parthenon temple in Greece in 1801. Greece has demanded their return, saying they were taken illegally. The marble statues are still on display in the British Museum. Many artifacts are now being returned to their homelands. They are important to help archaeologists fill in gaps in cultural knowledge and understanding. This knowledge helps keep a culture alive from one generation to the next.

There are many ongoing issues, such as war and **climate change**, that are of concern to archaeologists. In Syria, civil war has led to the destruction of countless archaeological sites. Museums have been looted and priceless treasures taken. On North America's Pacific coastline, cultural treasures are being threatened by rising sea levels, which are caused by climate change.

These ancient ruins of the city of Palmyra were destroyed during the Syrian civil war in 2015.

Conserving artifacts allows them to be used for ongoing research.

One Goal, Many Scientists

Preserving the past takes more than just uncovering and interpreting artifacts. Archaeologists often collaborate, or work together, as part of a team of experts. Conservators are specialists trained to preserve and restore fragile or damaged objects. They usually work in a lab.

Conservators use chemistry and other sciences to figure out how best to clean, protect, and conserve every artifact found in the field. Where an artifact is found determines how it is preserved. Artifacts recovered from saltwater environments, for example, will often crumble when they dry out in open air. Iron artifacts can last a few days to months before they are conserved. Leather, wood, and rope are **organic** materials. They can deteriorate in hours, and need to be conserved quickly.

The fossil of a 50-million-year-old three-toed horse.

From the Field: Dr. Sandra Olsen

Dr. Sandra Olsen is a **zooarchaeologist** from Kansas. Her focus is prehistoric horses and their relationship to early humans. Her work includes collaboration with a team of scientists from many different fields. Not all of them are archaeologists. Dr. Olsen analyzes the bones left behind. Other scientists on her team study traces of horsemeat residue left on pottery tools. Specialists called **geophysicists** do remote sensing to find evidence beneath the grounds surface. The group all work together to create a complete picture of the relationship between horses and humans in prehistoric times.

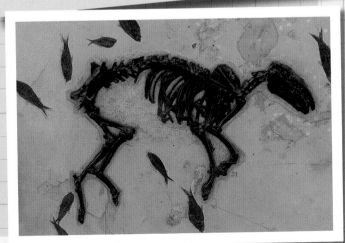

DIG IT!

Become a hands-on archaeology student!

Start with a Question

How does time and the usual weather in my community
affect artifacts that could be found there?

Step One: Create a "Dig" Site

Materials:

- 2 large plastic containers without lids
- Soil, small rocks, and sand (enough to fill the containers)
- 12 to 20 artifacts (make sure there is an even mix of organic—things that were once living—and inorganic materials). You could include an apple core, orange peel, leaves, paper, coins, paper clips, or pieces of broken plate.

1 Make a detailed list of the artifacts and organic materials you will bury. Write down the attributes of each item, such as size and color.

2 Add a layer of soil to the bottom of each container. Lay down several of the artifacts and bury them with soil.

3 Add a layer of rocks to each container. Lay down several more artifacts and cover them with soil. Lay down a few more artifacts and cover them with rocks. Continue alternating layers with artifacts until you fill the containers.

4 Once all artifacts are buried, put the plastic containers outside.

Step Two: Dig!

Materials:

- pencil, paper, and ruler
- small trowel
- paintbrush
- small mesh strainer

1 After two months, carefully dig your "site" by carefully removing soil and rocks 2 inches (5 cm) deep at a time, from one of the containers. Work in layers instead of digging holes. This means you remove rocks, sand, and soil across the entire surface of the container.

2 **Sift** removed soil through the strainer to make sure you don't miss any small pieces of artifacts or organic items.

3 Record everything you find by drawing it on a sheet of paper. Beside the pictures, write down contextual information, such as the exact location of the artifacts and any new or different attributes.

4 Set artifacts and organic items aside in a box and continue the excavation until you reach the bottom of your site.

5 After six months, repeat your dig with the other container. What differences do you notice in the condition of the artifacts and organic items from each container?

Step Three: Analyze and Interpret

1 Look at what you have uncovered. Compare it to the list of what you originally buried. How do the artifacts and organic items you found differ from the original list? Does the type of item (organic or inorganic) matter?

2 What was left unchanged?

3 Based on these findings, what do you think an archaeologist might find in a site left untouched for thousands of years?

Step Four: Communicate

1 Share your findings with your classmates.

2 Discuss what happened to the organic items.

3 Discuss how you think the environment might affect what archaeologists find. Do you think that dry climates would preserve artifacts better than damp ones? Why, or why not?

4 Discuss how this experiment could be repeated with a dry site and a wet site to test these theories.

PROJECTS AND DISCOVERIES

We are always learning about the past. The artifacts found and their analysis by archaeologists continue to expand our knowledge. More than 500 years ago, a storm sank the *Esmeralda*, a ship that was part of a fleet led by Portuguese explorer Vasco da Gama. In 2014, divers found a small bronze disc aboard the shipwreck in the Arabian Sea. They weren't sure what it was, until it was examined by a 3-D-imaging scanner. Faint marks on the disc proved that it was an astrolabe. This instrument was used to measure the height of the sun above the horizon at noon and helped sailors figure out their location.

This antique brass astrolabe shows how early Portuguese explorers traveled by sea.

This photo of Ta Prohm Temple in Cambodia shows the extent that vegetation can overtake and easily hide complete structures.

Seeing beyond the Trees

Researchers in Cambodia have carried out the largest airborne laser-scanning archaeological project to date. Using lidar, Australian archaeologist Damian Evans spent 10 years searching for evidence of an ancient industrial city in Cambodia called Preah Khan of Kompong Svay. Around 350 square miles (900 square km) of dense forest were scanned. Completed in 2015, the scans showed an almost 3-mile (5-km) by 3-mile (5-km) enclosed city in which the streets formed a grid pattern. Finding this hidden city proves that humans had a large impact on shaping their environments well before we had written records.

From the Field: Dr. Sarah Parcak

Dr. Sarah Parcak is founder of the Laboratory for Global Observation at the University of Alabama. She wrote the first textbook on **satellite** archaeology. She uses satellite images that reveal hidden sites lost over time. While mapping Egypt from her lab in Alabama, she discovered 17 unknown pyramids, 1,000 tombs, and 3,100 settlements. She is hoping this information will answer such questions as why the age of pyramid-building came to an end. Artifacts from these ancient sites are worth millions of dollars, and are being stolen and sold by thieves. She hopes satellite technology will also help archaeologists find and protect these tombs before they are looted.

Dr. Parcak wants citizens around the world to discover unknown archaeological sites. In 2016, she won a large award for her work. She is using the prize money to fund GlobalXplorer.org. It is a citizen-science platform that helps train people to find and protect heritage sites. Anyone with an Internet connection and a sense of curiosity can discover and protect ancient sites using satellite technology.

These pyramids in Giza, Egypt, are large and well-known, but there are many more archaeological sites in Egypt waiting to be uncovered.

GETTING INVOLVED

Field schools allow young people to get their hands dirty and get involved in archaeological work. Community archaeology projects are another introduction to this unique world of history and prehistory. Crow Canyon Archaeological Center in southwestern Colorado offers field-school programs. Visitors can sign up to take a tour of 1,000-year-old Pueblo Native American sites, work on a dig with an archaeologist, or assist in analyzing artifacts in the lab.

Kids can learn about archaeology at field schools.

Unite4Heritage

Many cultural resources are under threat around the world. The United Nations Educational, Scientific and Cultural Organization (UNESCO) is working to monitor and assess sites at risk, as well as protect museum collections from being looted and sold. These places, objects, and traditions make our world a rich and exciting place to live. More information can be found at: www.unite4heritage.org/en/

Go Online

There are countless archaeological sites and museums across the country and around the world that offer introductory programs for archaeology. You can also try out a virtual dig at Virtualmuseum.ca. Archaeologists are increasingly sharing more and more information online. One example of this is *From Stone to Screen*. It is a collaborative project to create a digital database of the archaeological teaching collections at the University of British Columbia. Check it out at http://cnerscollections.omeka.net.

Virtual Reality Saves the Day

There are times when archaeological treasures cannot be saved. In 1956, emergency research took place to record the archaeology of Glen Canyon in southern Utah before it was flooded for a hydroelectric dam. Eight years later, the area was underwater, covered by Lake Powell. Virtual exhibits can be built using archaeological data, however. These exhibits allow us to tour through archaeological sites. They are opportunities to experience the past as if we were walking directly through it.

The Iroquois were a powerful group of Indigenous American nations living in the northeastern United States and eastern Canada. They built long, narrow houses, called longhouses, where many families lived together. The Museum of Ontario Archaeology offers a virtual walk through a 16th-century longhouse using virtual-reality goggles. The experience brings archaeological discoveries to life with computer-generated images (CGI).

Interactive archaeological exhibits bring the past to life!

What Will Others Learn from Us?

Archaeologists uncover the remains of past lives. They discover tools people used, the foods they ate, and how they lived their lives on a daily basis. What things do you use in your daily life? What artifacts will you leave behind for future archaeologists to uncover? Do you think the job of future archaeologists will be more or less difficult because of the technology, such as computers, we have in our lives today?

LEARNING MORE

BOOKS

Huey, Lois Miner. *Children of the Past: Archaeology and the Lives of Kids.* Millbrook Press, 2017.

Malam, John. *Prehistoric Adventures: Stone Circles.* Wayland Publishers Ltd, 2017.

Shuter, Jane. *Excavating the Past: Mesopotamia.* Heinemann Library, 2016.

Wood, Alix. *Uncovering the Culture of Ancient Peru.* Powerkids Press, 2016.

Yasuda, Anita. *Archaeology: Cool Women Who Dig.* Nomad Press, 2017.

ONLINE

www.interactivedigs.com
Archaeological Institute of America's interactive dig site.

www.nps.gov/webrangers/activities/artifact/?id=02
The U.S. National Park Service Webrangers page includes games in which you can test your skills of deduction.

http://trowelblazers.com
Inspiring trowelblazing women in the fields of archaeology, geology, and paleontology.

PLACES TO VISIT

The Archaeology Museum, University of South Alabama
www.southalabama.edu/org/archaeology/museum
A showcase of artifacts from the Gulf Coast.

Canadian Museum of History, Gatineau, Quebec
www.historymuseum.ca
See the exhibit *From Time Immemorial: Tsimshian Prehistory.*

Museum of Ontario Archaeology
http://archaeologymuseum.ca
Discover the lost Lawson Village.

Penn Museum, Philadelphia
www.penn.museum
Explore amazing artifacts from Ancient Egypt and Greece.

Yukon Beringia Interpretive Centre
www.beringia.com
Uncovering the Ice Age.

GLOSSARY

analysis Detailed examination of artifacts or data

archive A collection of historical documents or records

artifact A physical object built, modified, or used by humans

attributes Qualities or characteristics an artifact may possess

bias To have preset beliefs and ideas

civilization Society, culture, and way of life in a particular area

climate change Global warming and other changes in weather and weather patterns resulting from human activity

conference A gathering at which experts discuss their work and share ideas and results

cultural resource Physical evidence or place of past human activity

culture The beliefs and behavior of a group of people

datum point A point that serves as a reference, or base, for the measurement of other things

domesticated Animals that have been tamed so that they can live with or be used by humans

evidence Proven facts that show a hypothesis may be true

evolution The gradual change of living things that takes place very slowly from one generation to the next

excavation Digging, recording, and interpreting the physical remains of people who lived in an area, in order to understand how they lived

field school A short program in which students learn from research done outside the classroom

fossil A bone, shell, or plant from millions of years ago, preserved as rock

funding Money made available for a particular project or investigation

geophysical The science of the physics of Earth

hypothesis An idea based on some prior evidence that could answer a question; it is a starting point for further investigation

industrial Having to do with factories and making things in large quantities

interpretation The act of figuring out what something means

journal A newspaper or magazine that deals with a particular subject or professional activity

migration The movement of people from one area to another

model An object or image used to show or explain an idea

mummy A preserved body, especially found in Egypt

organic Something that comes from living matter, such as plant material

paleoanthropologist A scientist who studies the origins and ancestors of today's humans using fossils and other remains

peer A person with the same level of education and experience working in the same field of science

prehistoric Belonging to a time before history was recorded in written form

radar A method of finding solid objects by sending and receiving reflected radio waves

satellite An body in orbit around Earth to collect information or for communication

sift To pass a substance through a mesh to get rid of lumps or large chunks

trade The exchange of goods between people

transit A tool used to measure horizontal angles

zooarchaeologist A person who studies what is left behind when an animal dies

INDEX

analyzing 10, 11, 12, 16, 18–19, 20, 23, 25, 26, 28
archives 6

battlefields 6, 20
bones 10, 13, 16, 19, 23
British Columbia 13

California 5
Cambodia 26
Canada 4, 5, 7, 29
carbon-14 11, 16
Carter, Howard 8
China 9
collaboration 23, 28
Colorado 28
conservation 22–23
context 16, 17, 19, 25
cultures 6, 9, 10, 22

datum point 14

Egypt 4, 8, 9, 27
England 5, 7, 21
Evans, Damian 26

field schools 28
fossils 9, 23

Greeks 6, 12, 22

hypotheses 10, 12, 13, 16, 19

Incas 6
Italy 12

Jones, Dr. Alexandra 21
journals 21

Kansas 23

labs 10, 18, 23, 27, 28
Leakey, Mary and Louis 9
lidar 15, 26

Machu Picchu 6
magnetometry 14
maps 15, 16
Massachusetts 19
metric system 16
Mexico 6, 18
museums 11, 20, 22, 28, 29

New Mexico 4

observation 10, 11
Olsen, Dr. Sandra 23

Parcak, Dr. Sarah 27
peer review 20
Peru 6
Petrie, Flinders 9
photographs 15, 16, 17
Pilgrims 19
Piltdown Man 21
pottery 9, 12, 14, 16, 18, 23
pyramids 27

radar 15
Romans 5, 6
ruins 7

satellites 27
scientific practices 4, 5, 10–11
Scotland 14
screens 16
settlements 5, 6, 11, 13, 19, 27
shipwrecks 4, 7, 26
statues 4, 22
stratigraphy 11, 15
surveys 14–15
Syria 22

Tanzania 9
Terracotta Army 9
tombs 8, 27
tools 13, 15, 29
trade 12, 17, 19

United States 16, 19, 29
Utah 10, 29

ABOUT THE AUTHOR

Megan Kopp has spent decades exploring the prehistory of the American Southwest. As an author of more than 80 published books, Megan's list of questions is long. What happened to the Ancestral Puebloan people? What stories do their rock art and stone dwellings tell? How can we help preserve these sites? When not writing in her office, Megan can be found exploring historic and prehistoric sites throughout Canada and the United States.